BLACKWOOD YESTERDAY

in photographs
including the villages of
WATTSVILLE, CWMFELINFACH, YNYSDDU,
PONTLLANFRAITH, OAKDALE, CEFN FFOREST,
FLEUR-DE-LYS, PENGAM, ARGOED,
MARKHAM AND HOLLYBUSH

Ewart Smith, M.Sc.

Foreword by
DON TOUHIG M.P.

Book 2

Old Bakehouse Publications

Abertillery

ISBN 1 874538 65 4

Published in the U.K. by
Old Bakehouse Publications
Church Street,
Abertillery, Gwent NP3 1EA
Telephone: 01495 212600   Fax: 01495 216222

Made and printed in the UK
by J.R. Davies (Printers) Ltd.

Foreword
by the R.H. Don Touhig M.P. for the Borough of Islwyn

We should be indebted to Ewart Smith for this, his second volume of Blackwood Yesterday. With the pace of life forever increasing in today's world, we tend all too infrequently to look back and reflect on what has gone before. Yet our history has shaped us and made us the sort of communities we are today. This is not to say we should live in the past, but we must learn from it.

In this volume we are reminded of our industrial roots in iron and coal, something I am personally conscious of as my own antecedents came to the Gwent valleys, as did many others, to work in the iron works in the early part of the last century. In pictures and words, Ewart Smith traces the lives of our forebears who inhabited Blackwood and nearby villages. Chapters on everything from education and religion to trade and entertainment give a flavour of what life was like. In some pages we can see in the faces of the people pictured, the struggles and sacrifices they endured and, in contrast, the lighter and happier times.

I am sure that everyone who picks up this volume will find it revealing and share my hope that others will follow later.

Don Touhig

October 1995

HOUSE OF COMMONS
LONDON SW1A 0AA

3

Contents

FOREWORD

INTRODUCTION

Chapter 1   BLACKWOOD TOWN

Chapter 2   THE SURROUNDING VILLAGES

Chapter 3   EDUCATION

Chapter 4   RELIGION

Chapter 5   TRADE AND INDUSTRY

Chapter 6   SPORT AND ENTERTAINMENT

Chapter 7   PEOPLE AND EVENTS

Introduction

It is more than two-hundred and fifty years ago (1738) since iron was first produced in this valley at Pont Gwaith y Hariarn, a mile or so north of Hollybush. It was produced there by two Breton metallurgists, probably because iron ore, limestone, a suitable fuel and abundant water were all available in close proximity. The chosen fuel was charcoal, made by burning the hardwood trees growing on the mountainside. Charcoal was preferred to coal since the government believed that coal produced too many poisonous gases! When Archbishop Coxe made a tour of the region at the beginning of the nineteenth century he commented that the region 'though rich in minerals, is supposed to be barren of objects either interesting or picturesque, and is therefore called the Wilds of Monmouthshire, and seldom travelled by the gentry, except for the purpose of grouse shooting. Impressed with the general prejudice, I neglected to explore it until my third tour'. On his third tour, of the Sirhowy valley he wrote 'The features of this vale are more wild and romantic than those of those of the Ebwy; it is narrower and deeper; and the shelving declivities, laid out in the meadows, stretch to the edge of the torrent, which roars in a profound abyss, obscured by overhanging trees'.

By the beginning of the eighteenth century, the mountainsides in the northern part of the valley had been completely denuded of their woodlands. Coal, when converted into coke, had become the preferred fuel for the ironworks. The days of the pack horses and mules treading their way to Newport on the mountains' ridges were soon to end. A lease dated 20 March 1800 enabled the founders of the Tredegar Ironworks (Samuel Homphray, Richard Fothergill and Matthew Monkhouse) to lay a tramroad from Tredegar to Pill, on the bank of the river Usk in Newport. Along this tramroad small mining villages were born at Hollybush, Argoed, Charlestown (that part of present Blackwood north of The Square), Blackwood, Pontllanfraith, Ynysddu and Cwmfelinfach. The production of iron and coal in the valley expanded rapidly and the insatiable demand for labour was met by an influx of workers from Gloucestershire, Somersetshire, Ireland and rural Wales. The South Wales Valleys developed a culture peculiar to themselves. A language (Wenglish) developed which was a mixture of Welsh and English. As a boy I remember using such words and phrases as: palaver (fuss and bother), twp (slow on the uptake), conflab (lengthy discussion), dab-hand (good at), chesty (arrogant, boastful), chopsy (talks a great deal), clecs (carries stories), cwtch (under the stairs), hec (hop), potch (mess about with), troughing (roof guttering), knock about with (keep company with), hammer and tongs (passionately loud), loshin (sweets), wonky (defective), crachach (top people in the area), and ashman (refuse collector).

As the decades passed deeper mines were sunk and new villages, which were now planned rather than allowed to evolve, were built at the beginning of this century - witness Oakdale, Markham and Wyllie. Blackwood became the business and commercial centre of the valley. It was well placed geographically in the centre of the valley and possessed a wider than average main street for a South Wales town. This was because the railway, which replaced the tramroad and had been opened to passenger traffic in March 1865, had been removed from the High Street and placed behind it on the east.

In the past few decades the mines have gradually closed, the coal dust has settled, the tips have been levelled and landscaped and a great deal of environmentally friendly light industry has come to the area. Though there is a vast amount of residential property, the area has been considerably beautified in recent years. In one sense some of the beauty of yesteryear is returning.

This book, the second in a series, is a small additional contribution to the history of the area, lest we forget that in this valley our roots lie in iron and coal. It contains some information connected with every decade in a form that can be easily understood by everyone.

CHAPTER 1

Blackwood Town

Entrance to Blackwood. 419

1. A view of the south end of Blackwood in the early days of the internal combustion engine. On the side wall of the house in the foreground H Rosser, a Hay & Corn Merchant advertises that he will also remove furniture. The whitewashed cottages to the right were demolished to make way for a garage. This is now the site of the Gulf petrol and service station.

2. The Square, Blackwood, taken from the east. The building shown here as Davies & Beynon was destroyed by fire in the early 1990s and has now been replaced by the Argos store. The railings to the left enclosed a well known town landmark - an underground gents toilet! The Bedwellty Urban District Council notice above the two men directs that anyone whose is aware of a fire should report it at Blackwood Police Station. At that time the station was in nearby Hall Street - a building which is now the home of Blackwood Rugby Club.

3.   An early photograph of the bottom end of the town. The large building on the left is the Parrot Hotel (named after a family not the bird!), which was used for all manner of public gatherings including religious meetings and dog shows. The Butchers' Arms (now the Porters) can be seen in the centre, and the first shop beyond the sunblinds is Cleaks. Two shops beyond Cleaks were demolished to widen the road at the top of Bridge Street. Caps and beards are much in evidence.

4.   Blackwood High Street at the top of Bridge Street. The grocer's assistant stands outside Scudamore's, the business to which the author's grandfather came as a baker towards the end of the last century. Those were the days! Gas lighting, muddy roads, shank's pony, a bicycle or a horse for transport.

BLW.21   HIGH STREET, BLACKWOOD

5. Blackwood High Street with one paperboy on a quiet Sunday morning in the 1960s. The three shops on the right are W Harris (sweetshop), E I Bebb (Butcher), and the Quality Cleaners. Across the gap (Gravel Lane) is the South Wales Argus Office.

High St. (3) Blackwood.

6. Looking north from the centre of Blackwood town on a date between the wars. Roberts the Printers is on the left, a baker's horse and cart opposite, while a van delivers Lovells Toffee Rex to Chappels' confectionery shop.

7.   William Street, which runs parallel to the High Street for the whole of its length, as seen from its south end in the 1920s. Mothers carry their babies wrapped in shawls, and several ash buckets are visible in the gutters awaiting collection by the local council.

8.   Park View Terrace, part of what is commonly known to locals as the upper part of Cefn Road. This terrace was built on the old road that led from the Rock and Fountain Inn at river level to Bedwellty Church. Road widening was going on continuously, this tree being well out into the road.

Blackwood. from The Graig. 1300.

9. A photograph of Blackwood from the east taken in 1920. Gordon Road runs directly to the sky line. There is one railway line in the foreground and another between William Street and the High Street in the middle distance. Between the High Street and Lilian Road are the spoil tips from the Lower Plas Colliery.

10. A pre-First World War photograph of Blackwood taken from the high ground behind Libanus School and looking northeast. The High Street runs diagonally from the right.

11. Looking at the southern end of Blackwood from the east in the mid 1950s. A van belonging to Brace, Bakers, Oakdale, is delivering to Maydwell's Shop. The prefabs, houses built soon after the end of World War II and intended to last for at most 25 years, can be seen in the centre near the skyline. Some are still in use in the Newport area.

12. The footbridge at the bottom of the steps near Sunningdale Nurseries. The remains of the centre pier of a former bridge stands in the foreground. This bridge was an important link for people having business on both sides of the river and is still in use today.

Yiew from Railway Line, Blackwood.

13. The view of Woodfieldside from the main road at Libanus. It shows the building of St David's Road.

BLW.17   FOUNDRY HILL, BLACKWOOD

14. Looking towards the Rock from the bend on the Foundry Hill in the mid 1960s. The photograph shows the line of the old road. The present road follows the curve of the railway line but is slightly to its left.

13

15. A photograph of the cenotaph at the top of Pentwyn Road c 1925 and before any trees were planted in the area.

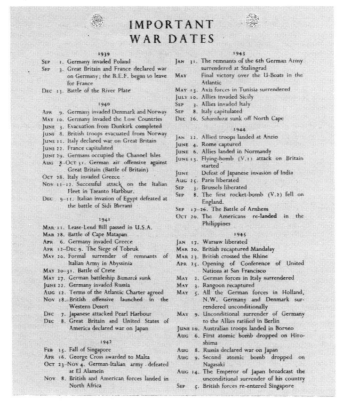

16. To commemorate the end of the war in 1945 every schoolchild was a given a copy of this calendar which gave the most important dates of the war. The other side of the card is shown in photograph 79.

Roll of Honour - Blackwood 1914-1918 War

W Baker	W G Hughes	H G Phillips
J Butler	R T Hutton	T Price
W J Carey	W D James	A E Roberts
O Coles	W Jeanes	W W Smith
J East	W J Jenkins	G H Snelgrove
O Ebdon	G P Jones	J H Spencer
A Evans	J W Jones	A R Stephens
G Firr	H S Lewis	R Stephens
J H Goodyear	S Lewis	W J Stokes
S Guest	A Meek	S Walton
W R Gwatkin	W Milton	L W Watkins
P J Gwilt	T J Morgan	A Williams
W G Halse	W J Nethercott	A Williams
S J Hambleton	H N Overton	T Williams
A J Harris		

Roll of Honour - Blackwood 1939-1945 War

A Abraham	W Harris	P Maynard
R G Bennett	C E Harrhy	W B Mountjoy
R Bray	I Harrhy	A R Parker
L Clayfield	A C Holvey	W J Parfitt
T Conolly	A Jones	N Perkins
H G Copping	E H Jones	L Petit
K Crewe	R Jones	V G Price
R Crewe	H Lee	S Salmon
V Ellway	S Lee	W G Thomas
D K Evans	R Legge	D Tiley
T Garrett	F Legge	T B Tomkins
A Gregory	A R Lewis	A Vernall
H C Griffin	M Maguire	L Wiltshire

17.   The names of those men from the Blackwood area who lost their lives serving King and Country during the two World Wars 1914-18 and 1939-45.

18./19.   Two houses, typical of the many that were built in the area as a result of John Hodder Moggridge's attempt to give the working population some independence and self respect. Moggridge should be thought of as the man who founded Blackwood. Each tenant was encouraged to build a cottage using money which had been loaned by Moggridge and would be repaid by regular instalments. Tenants had to pay an annual ground rent and were expected to cultivate their garden. These houses were situated in Hall Street (so named after Benjamin Hall, whose tramroad was quite near), a short distance from the High Street and, as the lower photograph shows, had no windows at the rear. They were built around 1830 and demolished in the mid 1950s. The row of houses behind is William Street.

Station Approach, Blackwood. 1304.

20. The only part of this scene that survives is the wall on the left which is now a boundary wall for Gibbons. The whitewashed Carpenters Arms was an important meeting house, situated opposite the railway station. Some businesses in nearby towns would not set up a business in Blackwood because the station was so far from the centre of the town. The pavement was raised at the station exit so that goods could be loaded onto a cart or into a van without lifting.

17

21./22. These pictures show the capping of an old mine shaft at the south western corner of the bus station site. This is all that remains of the Lower Plas Colliery.

23. The narrow railway bridge in Hall Street, Blackwood. It was built when the railway line was moved from the middle of the High Street to run behind it on the east side, in the 1860s. It was taken down and the road widened in the 1980s. The white building in the distance is the Capitol cinema. This cinema closed, was demolished and replaced by Kwik Save.

24. Joe and Olive Cobley in the garden of their home (c. 1920) adjacent to the present site of Kwik Save. Four gypsy caravans are visible in the background sheltered from the west by the railway embankment. The roof that can be seen in the distance belongs to the Palace Cinema - Babers the furnishers today.

The Surrounding Villages

25. A general view of the village of Wattsville taken from the west. There are many well cared-for allotments in the foreground.

26. A view of Cwmfelinfach from the South.

27. Maindee Road, Cwmfelinfach, looking towards Pontllanfraith. To the right is F N Silverthorn's shop.

28. A second look along Maindee Road, Cwmfelinfach, but this time in the opposite direction.

29. An old photograph of an early bridge over the Sirhowy river at Cwmfelinfach. The postage to send this card was ½d. The equivalent is about 1/5 p!!

30. The Pioneer Hotel, Cwmfelinfach, pre 1920, soon after the roof had been damaged in a storm. The man wears a waistcoat, leggings, a dai cap, and has the sleeves of his flannel shirt rolled up.

BRYNHYFRYD   CWM FELIN FACH

31. Brynhyfryd, Cwmfelinfach in 1908. Known as The Peacock House because of the topiary in the front garden.

32. A card of Ty Glan-y-nant, published by J Parfitt, Stationer and Tobacconist, Cwmfelinfach, in the early part of the century. This is adjacent to the gardens in the centre of the village.

33. A late 1950s photogragh of the Pensioners' Gardens, Cwmfelinfach, taken from the north east. The tip of coal spoil from Nine Mile Point Colliery dominates the view behind the Miners' Institute.

34. The bowling green at Cwmfelinfach.

Alexandra St., Ynysddu.

35. A typical 1920s view of Alexandra Street, Ynysddu. More than forty people are visible on the street. The children are playing, the women talking, the boys, some in short trousers, all wear caps. There is not a man in sight.

36. A general view of Ynysddu looking west.

37. A general view of Ynysddu looking towards the north east. The upper row of houses
shows the line of the old main road up the valley.

38. The view from Wyllie Colliery looking north. The village was built in 1927.

39. A picture of Wyllie Post Office taken soon after the Second World War.

40. The Council Office, Pontllanfraith, resplendent with its campanile in the days before the main road received its 'tarmac' surface, This building was the administrative centre of Mynyddislwyn Urban District Council.

41. Two beautifully built tunnels in dressed stone (long since gone) permit the river to pass under the railway line at The Falls, Pontllanfraith.

42.   The Tredegar Junction Hotel stands guard over the level crossing at Pontllanfraith when little more than horsedrawn vehicles caused the passage of trains any problem. An old man on his way to collect water, or possibly milk, stands chatting near the signal box.

Pontllanfraith Baths, Blackwood, Mon.

43.   The Outdoor Baths at Pontllanfraith, built by Mynyddislwyn U D C before the outbreak of World War II. It was the only Baths in the area and was much used by the schools. In the summer term children frequently walked from Blackwood to the Baths for swimming lessons. A single lesson would therefore take the whole morning - no National Curriculum then!

Pontllanfraith from the Hill. Nr Blackwood. 421.

44. This 1930 view of Pontllanfraith shows the Pontllanfraith Schools on the left with the road leading to Pentwynmawr on the right.

Pontllanfraith. General View.

45. A general view of Pontllanfraith, taken from within the grounds of St Augustine's Church in the middle 1930s, looking towards the Plough corner. In the foreground is an oil distribution centre, later to become a petrol service station.

46. This view of Pontllanfraith was taken by crossing the road on the previous photograph, and shows many of the same properties. It was taken many years earlier.

47. A photograph of The Villas in Blackwood Road, Pontllanfraith, taken during the first decade of the century. The man in the boater hat sports a prolific white beard while the man with a walking stick and bowler hat has a gold watch chain attached to the watch in his waistcoat pocket.

48. The view along Pentwynmawr High Street, in the direction of Newbridge, in 1921. H Morgan, a general provision merchant offers such washing aids as scrubbing boards and a tin bath.

49. The same High Street, 10 years earlier, but looking in the opposite direction. Morgans's shop is just along on the left. Note the condition of the road a little further on. The pavement is the place to stand and talk, but if you walk, the centre of the road is the place to be.

50. New Markham Crescent, Oakdale, soon after it was built, as evidenced by the very young trees that line the pavement.

51. An early photograph (1920s) of The Square, the centre of Oakdale village. The first shop belongs to Rosser & Thomas, grocers, selling Bourneville cocoa and Jacob's biscuits. Next door is West & Co the drapers store. The carefully planned village was built at some distance from the colliery. Work to clear the site for the colliery began in 1906, sinking the first pit shaft started the following year while housing and community building quickly followed. These included shops, an Hotel and Miners' Institute set around The Square, and a Cottage Hospital, opened in the summer of 1914, a short distance away with good views across the valley towards Blackwood.

52. The view of Oakdale colliery and village from the main road just north of Blackwood. Taken in the 1920s it shows the much older area of Rhiw Syr Dafydd in the valley and the new village of Oakdale high on the hill and some distance from the colliery stacks.

53. The view looking down Central Avenue towards the Primitive Methodist Church at about the time when the church was completed c 1917. This building is now called the Oakdale Christian Centre. The Oakdale Hotel is on the left while the Miners' Institute is still to be built on the right and tarmacadam has yet to appear on the road.

Croes Penmain. Nr Oakdale

Ernest J. Bush.

4032

54. Croes Penmain, Oakdale, c 1910. Long before the village of Oakdale was born this was one of the most important junctions in the area. Five roads met here. The road immediately ahead led to Manmoel and Penyfan, the one on the left to The Rock and Blackwood. The three roads coming into the picture from the foreground were from Pentwynmawr, Newbridge and Crumlin. The whitewashed building to the left is Gwesty Dirwestol - the Gwesty Inn, a building forced to convert to a coffee house because of Lady Llanover's desire (and authority!) to rid the area of the menace of strong drink. Also sited near this junction were the very necessary crafts of the blacksmith and the carpenter.

55. The Baptist Chapel in Markham Crescent, Oakdale. The building of this began in 1916.

The Bandstand, Oakdale, MON. 220

56. Oakdale had every modern amenity, as this 1920s picture of the bandstand suggests.

57. The Institute, Oakdale, pictured here in the early 1920s, opened on 10 September, 1917. The money to build it was loaned by the Tredegar Iron & Coal Company and repaid over a period of 25 years by contributions deducted from the miners' wages. It incorporated a reading room, library and billiards room, and became a focal point in the life of the village. The large hall was built later on the ground to the right and could be used as a cinema. When the building ceased to be needed by the community it was taken down and rebuilt at St Fagans, for the National Museum of Wales, as a permanent example of a Welsh Miners' Institute.

58. Rhiw Syr Dafydd bridge over the Sirhowy river. This single track bridge carries an inordinate amount of traffic between The Rock and Oakdale. It provides an important short cut for drivers coming down the Sirhowy valley and for those living at the north end of the town, to get to Crumlin and hence up the Abertillery valley or over to Pontypool.

MYNYDDISLWYN MOUNTAIN

59. Looking towards Mynyddislwyn Mountain from the west, c 1920. To the right is Islwyn Terrace. Mynyddislwyn Church is just off the picture near the horizon on the right.

The Square, Fleur-de-lis. 1942.

60.   One of the first cars seen in the area (Reg. No. L7904) stands outside the shops on The Square, Fleur-de-lys. Two well blooded butchers stand outside the business of J Crowe & Sons. Next door the draper (Morris?) advertises Jaeger Pure Wool. A gas light stands in the middle of the junction.

High Street, Fleur de Lis.

61.   Further along the High Street, and a few years later, the Trelyn Hotel (demolished a few years ago) faces some of the other shops in the village.

The Bridge,
Fleur-de-lis
& Pengam

62. The high bridge crossing the Rhymney river between Pengam and Fleur-de-lys. This picture was taken in 1925.

HIGH-ST-PENGAM

63. The view of High Street from Bont Chapel looking towards the Post Office corner c 1920. The Smiths is clearly visible beyond the School. The state of the road leaves much to be desired!

High Street, Argoed.

64. The High Street in Argoed (pre 1920), as shown on a photograph published by J Phillips, Stationer, Argoed. Note the original tramway running through the middle of the village.

65. The view, in 1920, from Manmoel Crossing looking south. To the right is Argoed station, with the village beyond, in the centre Cwm Argoed, above which is Oakdale colliery and the village on the distant skyline.

MKM 3   THE INSTITUTE, MARKHAM.

Copyright
Frith's

66. Another Miners' Institute, this time at Markham. Nowhere near as impressive a building as the one at Oakdale, but still a focal meeting point for the people of the village. The building has been re-roofed in recent years following a fire which seriously damaged it. It is still in use today.

67./68.   The interior of Markham Village Welfare Institute as it used to be. Every 'Stute' had a billiards room (snooker took over from billiards in later years), a library and a reading room.

Education

69. The 'temporary' building at Blackwood Junior School. This timber structure covered with corrugated sheeting was erected in the 1920s. It has been used both as a canteen and for teaching purposes depending on the need of the day. Like the prefabricated houses erected at the end of the last war this building was still in service long after its 'sell-by' date. It was finally demolished in 1995.

70. Blackwood Junior School looking spick and span in 1991. Up until Blackwood Secondary School was built (subsequently to become Blackwood Comprehensive School), this was where most children in the town remained until they left school.

71. Mrs Marion Evans with her flock at Blackwood Infants School in the 1980s.

72. Pupils at Blackwood Junior School in July 1963. Back row: Haydn Davies, Ian Coleman, Huw Jones, Carl Woods, Wayne Hicks, Andrew Morgan, Jacqueline Miles, Susan Balson, Denise Williams and Cheryl Richards. Second row: Jennifer Jones, Lynne Thomas, Kenneth Williams and Helen Beard. Front row: Cheryl Gibbs, Jane Wood, Susan Wake, Paul Anthony, Alan Meudell, David Shelton and Peter Chapman.

73.   St David's House, Ynysddu Junior School, c 1947. The headmaster, Mr Games, sits between Mr George and Miss E Williams.

74. St David's Day at Blackwood Infants School in 1970.

75. Scholarship Class, Blackwood Elementary School, 1946-47, the year of the big blizzard. The school was closed for six weeks because the boiler burst. Even when it had been repaired it could not be used because the coke used as fuel was frozen solid. As a result the 11+ examinations were postponed for several weeks. Headmaster (left) Mr Dick Lewis, and far right class teacher Mr Victor Norman.

76. Mrs Peggy Dash's class in 1977. Back row: left to right, Timothy Jones, Ian Jones, Kelvin Weaver, Gareth Lloyd, Mark Tovey, Richard Owen, David Smith and Michael Watkins. Second row: Kevin Williams, Maria Dzaleta, Helen Dalimore, Lisa Eugene, Michelle Haines, Tracey James, Deborah Burton and Thomas Rudge. First row: Ginina Minoli, Debra Berkley, Michelle Bird, Alison Hopkins, Mrs Dash, Michelle Meredith, Sandra Jackson, Rhianon Head and Victoria Bayliss. Front row: Ian Thomas, Andrew Lafferty and David Key.

77. Pupils at Libanus Junior School, Christmas 1947.

78. The cast of the Nativity Play at Blackwood School, Christmas 1974. Ceri Williams (Mary) and Granville Hemmings (Joseph) are surrounded by Wayne Johns, Sian Ballard, Julie Hands, Suzanne Summerill, Simon Wall, Kathryn Davies and Bryan Owens. Baby Jesus is played by Angelita!

79. At the end of the war in 1945 this message from King George VI was given to all schoolchildren.

8th June, 1946

TO-DAY, AS WE CELEBRATE VICTORY, I send this personal message to you and all other boys and girls at school. For you have shared in the hardships and dangers of a total war and you have shared no less in the triumph of the Allied Nations.

I know you will always feel proud to belong to a country which was capable of such supreme effort; proud, too, of parents and elder brothers and sisters who by their courage, endurance and enterprise brought victory. May these qualities be yours as you grow up and join in the common effort to establish among the nations of the world unity and peace.

George R.I.

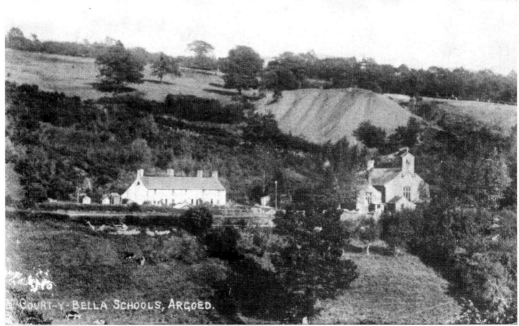

COURT-Y-BELLA SCHOOLS, ARGOED.

80. This postcard posted in 1918 shows the Court-y-Bella schools, as viewed from the west.

81. Lewis' School, Pengam, founded in 1729, as a result of the will of William Lewis, a bachelor, who had died at Gilfach Fargoed in the previous year. He owned much land and numerous collieries and lime kilns in the region. His will requested that fifteen poor boys from the local parishes be clothed and educated, and that sermons be preached by a lecturer, in the parishes of Bedwellty and Mynyddislwyn, every three weeks. This little acorn grew into one of the most prestigious schools in South Wales and for decades took more than thirty new boy entrants from the combined parishes of Bedwellty and Mynyddislwyn. The arrangement ceased in the early 1960s when comprehensive schools were introduced. This photograph was taken in the late 1930s.

82. Girls did not appear in the Edward Lewis story until the mid 1850s. In 1874 Lewis' School became a mixed school until the Higher Grade School at Pontlottyn was taken over in the late 1880s. A site was eventually selected for a new school at Groesfan, north of Bargoed, but after much lobbying it was decided to build at Hengoed. The Intermediate School for Girls, at Hengoed, was opened on 1st November 1900, and took girls from the parishes of Bedwellty and Mynyddislwyn on the same basis as boys went to Pengam.

83. Standard 1 pupils in front of the building covered by corrugated sheeting, at Ynysddu Infants School in the 1920s. One teacher, thirty-three pupils. Both boys and girls wear boots, few of which are in good condition.

84. Cwmfelinfach Infants Class, 1933. Teacher, Miss Alden. Back row: left to right, Unknown, A Jenkins, G Richards, J Williams, M McCullogh, J Brown, E Power, E Symons and A Booth. Middle row: J Lloyd, Unknown, C Bunce, E Warwick, Unknown, I Davies, C Crabb, K Powles, H Sheldon, B Roberts, Unknown. Front row: M Turner, D Jenkins, J Collins, A Hodinott, R Brown, M Radford, G Kear, D Gilchrist, N Butcher, D Boyd and R Nichols.

85. Staff of Pontllanfraith Grammar Technical School in 1965, just prior to becoming a comprehensive school. The headmaster is Mr E J Maguire.

86. Class 5, Cefn Fforest Junior School, Blackwood, in 1967. The headmaster is Mr D T Williams and the class teacher Mrs Mary Roberts.

CHAPTER 4

Religion

The Central Methodist Chapel, Blackwood, Built 1923.

87. The Central Methodist Chapel, Blackwood, with the Wesley Hall behind. This fine building, built at a cost of £12 582 17s. 2d., was opened on Thursday, 1 March 1928 (in spite of the date on the card!). It was the fourth chapel on this site, the third having been destroyed by fire on the evening of 23 November 1915. The chapel could seat 760 people on two levels. In recent years the levels have been separated. The upper level is now used for religious services, and the lower level for social and other gatherings.

88. Members of Blackwood Central Methodist Church, Whitsun 1920. Standing: Will Coleman, Tom Coleman, G H Coggins, Ray Coleman and Peter Coleman. Front row: Master Austin Fox, L G Coleman, George Coleman, Jethro Coleman, W C Woodward and Joseph Hendy (in front).

89. Rev E Tegryd Davies with a group of Trustees and Officers of the Central Methodist Church, Blackwood, in 1934.

90. A Christmas children's choir in the Central Methodist Church, Blackwood, before the major reconstruction that turned it into two separate floors. To the right are Haydn Panes (organist) and Gordon Bennett (choirmaster). The minister is Rev F S Pritchard.

Wesleyan Methodist Chapel, Blackwood, Built 1898.

91. This photograph shows the third Wesleyan Methodist Chapel to be built in Blackwood. The first was built near St Margaret's Church, had 100 seats, and was used as a place of worship for the period 1834-1861. By 1861 it was found to be too small, so Lewis Lewis, the Tyisha landlord was approached and agreed to sell the Methodists a plot of land in the centre of the town adjoining The Square. The doors and windows were a gift from a friend of John Waters. He brought them over from Bristol but all the stone was quarried locally by voluntary labour. By the late 1890s it was agreed that this second church was also too small and so a third building (the one seen in the photograph) was erected. This was in use from 1898 until it was burnt down in 1915.

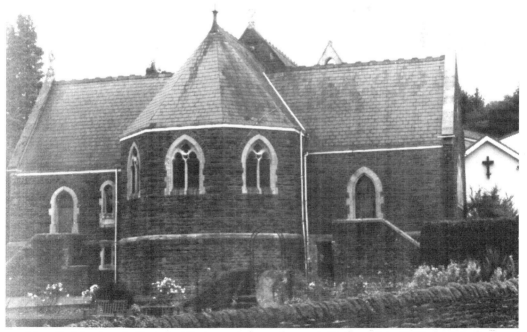

92. St Margaret's Church, Blackwood, from the east. Dedicated to St Mary of Antioch, the church was built in 1876, extended by building the present chancel in 1891, and had a choir vestry added in 1960. The first priest in charge was Matthew Moggridge a descendant of John Hodder Moggridge who founded the town. The most recent addition, a new church hall, was built to replace the former hall which stood in Hall Street on the site opposite Islwyn Crystal.

93. The interior of Penmain Chapel when it was taken over by Mynyddislwyn Male Voice Choir as their rehearsal room. The evidence as to how well it had been cared for is here for all to see.

Penmain Independent Chapel, the second non-conformist church in Wales was founded by Henry Walter in 1694. Walter had been an executor of William Wroth's will and it was Wroth who had founded the first non-conformist church at Llanvaches a short time previously. The first non-conformist building in Wales was the chapel built at Penmain in 1694. The first minister after the chapel was built was John Harris. There was much enthusiasm for non-conformism in this sparsely populated agricultural community and by 1717 the membership had reached 250. During the period 1710 - 1837 there were just three ministers, the longest serving being Dafydd Thomas who was minister at the church for 50 years (1787-1837). John Jones was assistant minister when Dafydd Thomas died and by 1839 a rift in the church had become so serious that a small group, led by John Jones, broke away and set up a rival church at Jerusalem, nearer Blackwood, but still on the Mynyddislwyn side of the Sirhowy river.

In 1887/8 Penmain was completely rebuilt at a cost of £700 and was reopened on Sunday 27 May 1888. The last service was held at Jerusalem on 3 July 1977 after which the few surviving members returned to Penmain, bringing the total membership there to about a dozen. An important 17th century oak communion table was given to the Welsh Folk Museum at St. Fagan's in April 1982. The last service at Penmain Chapel was held on 25 January 1990 when there were 5 members present. A few years later the building was bought by Mynyddislwyn Male Voice Choir as their base. Subsequently it has been repaired and brought up to date so that there is every hope that the building will continue to contribute to the life of the community for years to come.

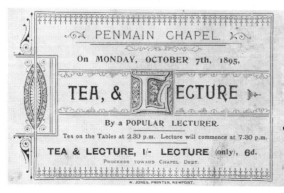

94. The ticket for a Tea and Lecture at Penmain Chapel in 1895. It was obviously an important gathering since Tea was 'on the table at 2.30 p.m.' but the lecture did not start until 7.30 p.m. The cost of 6d (2½p) for the tea and 6d for the entry to the lecture would appear to be quite expensive when the change in the value of money is taken into consideration.

95. Major restoration was necessary to the outside of Penmain Chapel to make the structure safe. This picture shows one of Terry Carpenter's men rebuilding a section of the south side wall.

96. The Primitive Methodist Church, Oakdale, founded in 1914, but shown here as it was in 1920. It is the dominant feature if you stand outside the Oakdale Hotel and look down Central Avenue.

97. Courtybella Church, Argoed, in the 1950s. This church served the Anglicans of Oakdale until a building made of timber and corrugated sheeting was erected at the bottom of Central Avenue in 1921. Today, this building is used as the church hall, a new church having been built on the opposite side of the road. This picture shows Sunnyview, Argoed in the background.

98. The Methodist Church, Wyllie, in 1949. The building was modelled on the mother church at Blackwood.

99. Ebenezer Baptist Chapel, Pengam in the mid 1920s. A horse and carriage is crossing the bridge over the Rhymney river on its way to the crossroads at Pengam School.

100. St Augustine's Church, Pontllanfraith, in the days long before it became enveloped by trees. The first half of the church (the back) was built in 1870, the second half (the front) around 1923 and a new porch added in 1995.

101. One of the oldest churches in South Wales and one of the few comparatively untouched since it was built in the thirteenth century. The church was enlarged and the tower added in the fourteenth century. The oldest part is the chancel. Some of the old stonework is most interesting.

102. A recent view of the interior of Bedwellty Church looking from the south door towards the chancel.

103./104. Close detail of the left hand side panels of the Tudor chest shows the pierced heart, hands and feet of Jesus in the upper panel. In the lower panel are three nails on a shield, together with a scourging whip, a hammer and a spear.

105. The front of the fifteenth century Tudor vestment chest in the chancel of Bedwellty Church. The great skill of the craftsman of the time, who used the most basic of tools, is still much in evidence.

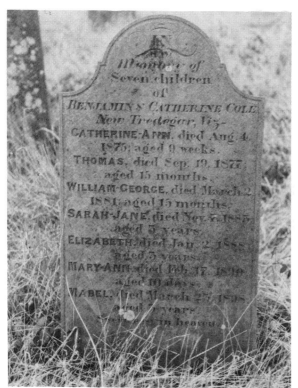

106. A very touching tombstone to be found on the southwest side of Bedwellty Church. It records the deaths of the seven children of Benjamin and Catherine Cole of New Tredegar. All seven died between 1875 and 1898, the eldest being but 5 years old. What tragedy struck that home.

107. This photograph of the north wall of Bedwellty Church shows part of the extensive strengthening that has been carried out in recent years to combat the effect of movement caused by underground colliery workings.

108. One of the oldest recorded ages in the area. Catherine Dillin died in 1859 at the remarkable age of 110.

109. William, the son of Morgan and Mary Thomas, who was far better known by his bardic name of Islwyn, was born in Ynysddu (the black island) in April 1832. He was educated at Cowbridge Grammar School. His father wanted him to follow his elder brothers and become a mining surveyor, but unfortunately, his father died just before these decisions had to be made.

As a consequence of the influence of his brother-in-law he decided to enter the ministry of the Calvinistic Methodists. To train for this he left for Swansea where he met and fell in love with a beautiful young lady by the name of Ann Bowen, but just before she and William (now 21) were to be married, she died. Although he married Martha Davies from Swansea some eleven years later it is believed that he never really got over the death of his beloved Ann. It is said that he was the finest Welsh poet of the nineteenth century. His great philosophic poem was called 'Y Storm'. He took his bardic title Islwyn (the voice of the wind or the storm) from the name of the mountain he could look out on. His two great loves appeared to have been nature and children. For many years he was involved in editing Welsh poetry for numerous magazines and newspapers. In November 1878, he died childless, at the young age of 46.

110. A large gathering at Ynysddu for the laying of the foundation stone for St Theodore's Church on 23 September 1925. The local PC stands in the foreground to check that all is in order, while a bus chugs along on the main road.

111. The last days of the Church Hall (c 1974) situated in Hall Street, Blackwood. A sizeable building, it had a stage and was large enough to put on plays and pantomimes. Although near the centre of the town, it was too far from St Margaret's Church. Accordingly it was demolished in the 1970s when a new Church Hall was built adjacent to the church.

112. Argoed Baptist Chapel from the east. The first chapel on this site was erected in 1817. It was rebuilt in 1851, a vestry added late in the last century, and renovated, including the addition of heating apparatus and gas lighting, in 1913.

113. The mainly whitewashed hilltop church of St Tudor's, Mynyddislwyn, before the roof structure was changed quite dramatically to give its present day look. As was customary, most old churches were whitewashed.

114. A pre-1920 photograph of New Bethel Chapel, on the road from Pentwynmawr to Mynyddislwyn Church.

CHAPTER 5

Trade & Industry

115. Oakdale Colliery from the north west. This early picture shows three sets of pithead gear and a single tower with a square cross-section.

116. View of the colliery surface, Oakdale, looking northwards from the top of No 2 chimney stack in 1939.

117. HRH Princess Margaret with Mr (later Sir) Alfred Nicholas when she visited the South Wales Switchgear factory, Pontllanfraith, on Thursday, 2 November 1950.

South Wales Switchgear

South Wales Switchgear began operations at its new Pontllanfraith factory in 1946. Switchgear products were transferred there from the original Treforest factory (Switchgear and Inventions Ltd was taken over in 1941) allowing the manufacture of Power Transformers to begin at Treforest, and continue there to the present day. Switchgear was allowed to develop at Pontllanfraith, ultimately throughout the voltage ranges 440V to 132000V. The company was set up under the umbrella of Aberdare Cables, a company pioneered in 1937 by Sir George Usher, F G Penny and later Sir John Pascoe, eventually becoming part of the Aberdare Holding Group of Companies. At that time it was considered very dubious to attempt to introduce a high tech industry in an area of high unemployment which was sadly lacking in technical skills. Thanks to the belief and drive of Alfred Nicholas (later Sir Alfred) who was appointed Managing Director in 1942, the initial problems were overcome and the business flourished. The coal and steel industries were contracting and few businesses from England, apart from munitions, were willing to set up in an area that was so lacking in skilled labour. In these early days, South Wales Switchgear wanted to manufacture a product calling for a high degree of skill with an untrained and unskilled work force. Their solution was to create a skilled work force by training their own apprentices. A small number of engineers and technologists were brought in, mainly from the north of England, and about a dozen young men from the local grammar and technical schools were taken on as the first batch of apprentices. As more young men became skilled, the company and the apprenticeship scheme expanded until, by 1960, the company was taking on about 120 new apprentices a year. Records show that in 1962 out of a total work force of almost 3000 employed on six sites in South Wales and one in Scotland (there were also seven factories overseas), nearly 600 of them were apprentices at the Blackwood and Treforest plants. Much encouragement was also given to Commonwealth and other overseas students to come to Pontllanfraith to be trained. Such contacts were to have added value when the students returned to their home countries and took up responsible jobs which sometimes included purchasing South Wales Switchgear's products.

During World War II there were many Government contracts. In particular the Admiralty entrusted numerous prestigious orders to the newly formed company. Many Royal Navy ships were equipped with South Wales Switchgear products but there would be a serious problem as soon as the war was over. When the war finished there were about 300 employees, approximately 80% of whom were ex-miners who had left the mines for health and other reasons. The immediate need as soon as the war had ended was for domestic products. From 1946 wash boilers, laundry units, electric cookers, immersion heaters, house service panels and drying cabinets were produced to satisfy the insatiable demand for these products in the immediate post-war years. In 1947 switchgear manufacture began at Pontllanfraith, and it was local councils that were to play a significant part in the development of the company's early products for use in the electricity supply industry. The first peacetime equipment supplied by the company was an 11,000-volt oil circuit breaker to Tredegar U.D.C. Other orders quickly followed from the councils at Bedwellty, Cardiff and Caerphilly. As the years passed higher voltage switchgear was developed and an active sales force began to sell across the length and breadth of this country and the world. In the early 1950s large contracts were being converted from basic design (in a drawing/design office that was the largest in Wales) to completion on site, in record time.

A contented work force is essential to a successful company. In order to achieve this the management encouraged a full programme of social activities. The social club catered for sports such as football, rugby, cricket, swimming, table tennis, darts, angling and small bore rifle shooting as well as photography. In many sports the company teams competed successfully in the local leagues. There was also a very active engineering society providing lectures and discussion groups on a wide range of engineering topics. Christmas was an important time in the life of the company. Christmas parties were held for customers' and employees' children and departmental parties were organised for the employees. Without question the high point of the festivities was Father Christmas, on his sleigh drawn by six reindeer, followed by a party of choristers. A prearranged route at advertised times resulted in the tableau bringing joy to thousands of children and their parents. Visits were made to hospitals, children's homes and old people's homes. The sizes of the crowds testified to the success of this annual event.

In the 1960s trading conditions at home and abroad worsened forcing the company, like many others, to contract and in 1973 it was absorbed into the Hawker Siddeley Group. This breathed new life into the company and times improved, so much so, that in 1978 they received The Queen's Award for Export Achievement. In 1990 the Hawker Siddeley Group was taken over by the conglomerate British Tyre and Rubber (BTR). Eventually, in 1992, South Wales Switchgear combined with Brush Switchgear of Loughborough, another Hawker Siddeley Company to form Hawker Siddeley Switchgear. Since that date many changes have taken place resulting in the work force decreasing to about 260.

118. Taken in 1991, on the retirement of Colin Donovan (extreme right), this photograph shows ten former apprentices, each with more than 40 years service. Back row: Richard Davies, Bernard Treasure, Peter Gay and John Matthews. Front row: Alan Price, Keith Mudford, Harry Martin, John Richards, Edward Jones and Harold James.

119. South Wales Switchgear's Annual Staff Dinner Dance at the Park Hotel, Cardiff, in the early 1960s.

120. The Sales Engineering Typing Pool of South Wales Switchgear in 1961, under the expert control of Yvonne Dight (front right).

121. A selection of girls employed at South Wales Switchgear in 1967, dressed in Welsh costume to celebrate the 25th Anniversary of the company, with their boss, Sir Alfred Nicholas. This idea was used on numerous occasions when presenting the company to potential foreign buyers. Back row: Diane Lloyd (Sales), Ann Williams (General Manager's Office), Mary Hughes (Drawing Office) and Edna Jones (Drawing Office). Front, Kneeling: Pam Williams (Material Control) and Marilyn Lane (Works Manager's Secretary).

122. Markham Colliery with the village of Hollybush in the background. The picture shows well, how the road snakes up the valley. The colliery was named after Sir Arthur Markham, MP for Mansfield, Nottinghamshire (1900-16), who was a popular figure in that area, and was associated with the Liberal Party, and a director of the Tredegar Iron & Coal Company. The colliery belonged to a subsidiary of the T.I.C. It was opened in 1912, linked to Oakdale in 1979 and closed in 1985.

123. The remains of Llanover Colliery, Argoed, in the early 1960s. The site is to the east of the main Blackwood-Tredegar road and is visible from this road just below Manmoel Crossing.

124. Construction of the pithead baths at Wyllie Colliery, nearing completion in 1949.

125. The staff at The Washery at Oakdale Colliery in 1926.

126. Wyllie Colliery - opened by the Tredegar Iron and Coal Company in 1926, the year of the General Strike, and closed by the National Coal Board in 1967/8. A village was built adjacent to the mine, and the community buildings, in particular the Miners' Institute, resulted in the creation of a very strong community spirit.

127. A group of miners at Wyllie Colliery.

128. Burnyeat Brown's Coronation Colliery, Ynysddu, in the first decade of this century.

129. Times were bad in the area during the General Strike of 1926. This photograph shows local miners digging for outcrop coal.

130. This photograph, which has been sent from America, shows the work force employed by Albert Barnett on a site opposite St Augustine's Church, Pontllanfraith. He is described as a wheelwright, undertaker and funeral furnisher. The number of people employed would suggest that it was a thriving business. Today, the site is occupied by Blackwood Building Supplies - see next photograph.

131. The same site as shown in picture 130, but in more recent times.

132. Thomas Ellis, whose father had been at Penydarren, Merthyr when Trevethic had operated his locomotive from Penydarren to Abercynon in 1804, was appointed chief engineer at Tredegar Iron Works in the mid-1820s. In 1828 he assembled a George Stephenson steam locomotive, named Britannia, that had been delivered to the Tredegar Works in pieces. Both Thomas and his wife are buried at Bedwellty church. This photograph shows the grave of his wife Ann.

133. Blackwood Station looking north towards The Rock. Originally the Sirhowy Tramroad, the line was re-routed during the period of the Sirhowy Railway Company (1860-1875). A passenger service from Sirhowy (Tredegar) to Newport was inaugurated on 19 June 1865. The station buildings in the photograph date from 1876-78. The line through Blackwood was taken over in turn by the London North Western Railway, London Midland and Scottish Railway and finally by British Rail under nationalisation until it closed in 1960.

134. The last train leaves Rhiw Sir Dafydd, near Oakdale Colliery, in May 1990. It is travelling south.

135. A railway employee leaning against one of the moveable gates of the level crossing at Pontllanfraith top station.

136. Pontllanfraith Low Level station in the 1950s. The line led to Pontypool. All that remains of this view is St Augustine's Church, shown in the centre of the photograph.

137. This view, looking north, of a train at Argoed station (built in 1878) shows the three tracks, a well carved verandah and the beautifully cut eaves of the station building. Houses in Penylan Road rise to the skyline above the signal box.

138. A single carriage passenger train on the up line at Wyllie station. The colliery baths are in the background.

139. Hollybush station at the begining of the century. The original station was about a mile north of this point and served the Old Hollybush Colliery (1870-1921) and the New Hollybush Colliery (closed 1914), two collieries owned by E D Williams of Maesruddud. The passenger service of the line from Risca to Nantybwch used this station and was withdrawn on 13 June 1960.

140. The Coach & Horses Inn, Blackwood, shortly before demolition in 1958. This was the most important meeting place in the town at the time of the march on Newport by the Chartists. Note the window that had been blocked up to avoid paying the window tax on it. Chartist House now stands on the site and bears a plate indicating the significance of this spot.

Bedwellty Urban District Council.

FIRE GUARD SERVICE.

To *Miss E Lewis*

IN THE YEARS
1940 TO 1944.

when our homes were in grave danger from air attacks you freely gave of your time and skill to the cause of Civil Defence Service

from *1943*

to prepare yourself ready to combat fire and to save life and property at the risk of your own whenever and wherever your services were required.

The Chairman and the Members of the Council appreciate your generous service and the great contribution you made in the defence of your homeland.

May you find success in your work, happiness in your leisure and be guided by a living memory of your

FIRE GUARD SERVICE.

W A Harris
Clerk.

W E Hemmings
Fire Guard Officer.

F Salway.
Chairman of the Council.

J J Paues
Chairman of the Fire
Guard Committee.

141. During the last world war every able bodied adult was expected to make a contribution to the war effort. Typically this meant belonging to organisations such as the Home Guard, Ambulance Service, Police Specials or ARP (Air Raid Precautions). This 'Thank You' certificate was presented to the person named after hostilities had ceased.

142. Taken in the 1950s, this is one of the last 'corner shops' in Blackwood - that of E Maguire in William Street. Many of these shops were the converted front rooms of private dwellings. In William Street there were four such shops, all now restored as private houses.

143. C E Longstaff's Noted Penny Bazaar, situated where Supercigs the newsagent and sweet shop is today, was packed with odds and ends. Belonging to a Cardiff firm, in the early days every item on sale cost one penny (1d), that is less than ½p today. The business closed in the late 1950s when it became Bebb's the butchers.

144./145. The George Hotel, Blackwood, before and after the alterations to its frontage.

146. One of the oldest public houses in the town still in use today. Shown here as the Tredegar Arms the name has reverted in recent times to its original name, The Flour Mill. The ground floor window on the side wall used to be the entrance to Bounds & Sons, men's hairdressers in the town for many years. The trees behind have grown on the site of The Rink, the social mecca of the town until the late 1930s.

147. The Star Supply Stores, one of the many grocers on Blackwood High Street in 1912. The premises are now occupied by Nerfertiti.

148. A man nicknamed 'Squash' stands in the doorway of Adams & Son, Grocers and Provision Merchants, Ynysddu. The message on the reverse of the card is written in English but is concluded in Welsh.

149. The 400 year-old mill at Gelligroes, from the south west, in the early 1970s. The building is now used as a candle factory. David Constable's company, Candle Makers Supplies, took over the building some seven years ago after moving from premises in London. He has sold candles to many famous people including Prince Charles and made the world's largest free-standing candle which reached a height of 30 feet.

150. A Victorian letter box (note V R at the top) still in use today. It is housed in a west wall of the Old Mill.

151. Archibald Willis, a Blackwood baker, stands with his horse and delivery cart. Note the bread basket at the front. He emigrated with his family to Ontario, Canada in the early 1920s.

152. A Griffin bus, on the Blackwood-Crumlin route, standing outside Suter & Bailey Ltd the furnishers on Blackwood High Street in the early 1950s. To the left is the Embassy Cafe and ballroom and to the right the Welsh Dry Cleaners.

153. A West Mon bus makes it through the railway arch halfway up Aberbargoed Hill. The buses had special engines because the hill was so steep, and carefully selected drivers who were paid a small additional wage. The driver had to know exactly how far to drive through the arch before pulling sharply to the right, otherwise the bus would not get through.

154. Formerly a blacksmith's shop, situated just south of The Rock public house, this building has been converted into residential accommodation in recent years.

CHAPTER 6

Sport & Entertainment

155. An important event at Oakdale Bowling Club in 1921. A large gathering was present, including two ladies, for the presentation of the Express Cup to J Birks.

156. Blackwood Rugby Club's First XV for the away match against Kenfig Hill during their first season in the Heineken League in the 1990-91 season. Back row, left to right: Simon Williams, Lyndon Rees, Gavin Thomas, Martin Barber and Geraint Hughes. Middle row: Crayson Williams, Neil Turley, Mark Hodges, Alan Hughes, Richard Lewis, Neil Coles, Glenn Mahoney and Chris Davies. Seated: Lennie Graves, Paul Fletcher, Robert Tomsa, Mark Thomas (captain), Neil Barber and Andrew Royall.

157. Pontllanfraith Grammar School, 1st XV, 1935-36. Standing, left to right: Mr Rees, Mr H Jones, D G Rees, L Howells, R Harwood, D Thomas, C Trott, C V Jones, A Edwards and Mr Bowen (Headmaster). Seated: H Lloyd, K Egan, F Lease, I Morris (Capt.) T Bowditch, D Burch and R Richards. In front: R Thomas and K Richards.

Although the school first started to play rugby in 1932, this is the oldest known photograph of a school rugby team.

158. Pontllanfraith Grammar School First XV, 1955-56. Back row: Carl Thomas, Bob Williams, Philip Jones, Dawson Phillips, Derrick Mills and Mike Ellis. Middle row: Mr Roy Hunt, Mike Price, Byron Farr, George Jenkins, David Evans, Robert Dredge, Geoff Morris and Mr Capwell (Deputy Head). Front row: Robert Llewellyn, David Jenkins, Byron Thomas (captain) Dennis Harris and David Moore.

159. Oakdale Colliery, first Interdepartmental Rugby Match 1948/49. Standing: unknown boy, Dennis Perrott (boy), Jack Edwards, Bill Heaton, Dennis Jones, Bernard Heaton, Arthur Powell and Les Lucas (Referee). Seated: Austen Perrott, Bob Owen, Harry Cartwright, Jock Johnson, Bill Brain, Ossie Barnes, John Thomas, Cecil Watts, Doug Bosley and Gordon Hardwicke.

160. Blackwood Tennis Club, Welsh Division 3, 1973. Standing: Peter Roberts, Chris Grey and B Dimambro. Seated: Peter Phillips, David Jones, Geoff Morris (captain) and Geoff Davies.

161. In the late 1960s a sixth form pupil who passionately wanted to play first team rugby for Lewis' School, Pengam, was politely told by his PE teachers, Mr Bryn Jones and Mr Davies, that he was too small to make the grade and the best thing he could do was to turn to athletics. This advice turned out to be the best advice he could have been given for it led to his introduction to hurdling; to specialising in the 110 metres hurdles, and eventually to representing his country at the Olympic Games on two occasions. That young student was Berwyn Price, a name well known to anyone in Wales the least bit interested in athletics. His subsequent achievements say it all.

He represented Great Britain twice in the Olympic Games - Munich 1972 and Montreal 1976 when he was Captain of the Great Britain Athletics Team; three times in the European Championships - Helsinki 1971, Rome 1974 and Prague 1978; and Wales four times in the Commonwealth Games - Edinburgh 1970, Christchurch 1974; Edmonton 1978 (where he was Commonwealth Games Champion and Captain of the overall Welsh Team) and Brisbane 1982. Most of Berwyn's working life has been spent with Swansea City Council where he is now Assistant Director of Leisure Services. He has numerous honorary posts concerned with sport and still keeps fit enough to run in the 1994 and 1995 London Marathon to raise funds for the Welsh Sports Aid Foundation. Other highlights were taking part in the European Junior Championships in Paris 1970, the World Student Games in Moscow 1973 and the European Indoor Championships (Silver Medal) 1976.

162. Jack Gardiner's collie Shan, or more fully, Champion Coverdale's Lady Shan. Bought from Len Green's Coverdale Kennels, Pontyclun, as a pet for his daughters Linda and Sharon, this bitch proved to be the best bitch ever bred by those kennels. Her first big win was at Crufts in 1959 and she was awarded her third challenge certificate at the West of England Ladies' Kennel Society show when just 3½ years old. As they say in the breed this 'made her up'. From then on she was entitled to be called a champion dog.

163. Early closing day in Blackwood was Thursday. This 1920s photograph shows Blackwood Thursdays' Association Football Club in a varied selection of jerseys.

164. Cwmfelinfach Wednesday A.F.C. 1911-12. Back row: left to right, T Harris, G Goldsmith, A Long, B McAnally and H Thomas. Second row: N Richards, J Price, W Samuels (Vice-President), W Williams, E Probert, G Tudor, E Spearing, L Bassett, T Smith, H E Coles (Vice-President) and J Jones (Trainer). Third row: Jack Davies (Hon Sec), L Prosser, T Taylor (Captain), Mr John Hughes D C (President), R Hutchinson (Vice-Captain), T A Parry and A E Waldron (Hon Treasurer). Bottom row: F Lee, T Donnelly, W Gwilym and C Gooch.

165. A 1920s soccer club pose with their trophies outside the Pioneer Hotel in Cwmfelinfach.

166. The team representing Ynysddu Albion A F C before taking the field, sometime during the First World War, to play in a game 'in aid of winter comforts for their comrades at the front'.

167. Ynysddu Soccer Club for the 1910-11 season. Men's headgear was important. The norm was a cap, but the most desirous headgear was a bowler hat. A posh waistcoat was also the height of fashion.

168. Blackwood Comprehensive School's Trampolining and Gymnastics Team 1974. Standing: Mrs Jean Burland, Carol Pask, Susan ?, Unknown and Mr Tony James. In Front: Neal Prosser, Susan Chidgey, Tony Williams, Unknown and Nigel Teague (Welsh under 13s trampoline champion and Gwent's first Schools' Champion).

169. Blackwood Comprehensive School's Soccer Team, 1979-80. Winners of the Ivor Tuck Cup 1982-83. Standing: Simon Williams, Noel Watkins, Stephen Finch, Craig Bruzas, Mark Watkins and Mr Arthur Morgan (coach). Seated: Richard Pask, Rhodri Lloyd, Simon James, Lyndon Symonds (Welsh cap), Neal Leonard, Ian Phillips and Shane Hall.

170. Combined rugby teams at Blackwood Comprehensive School for the 1972-73 season. The headmaster, Mr Jack Powell is flanked by Brian Hardwick (on his right) and Tony James.

CHAPTER 7

People & Events

171. Members of the Penllwyn Glee Society in 1929. One of their trophies stands proudly in front of their conductor.

172. Wyllie Glee Party in 1932. The conductor, Mr F C Edwards is seated between the guest artistes Gwladys Cooke and Mary Thomas.

173. The children of Wyllie village in a production of Marietana in 1929. The performance was given in a large marquee, on the ground where the chapel was built in 1932. The boy kneeling on the right is Eddie Evans. He was an excellent pianist and was attached to the Wyllie Glee Party until he was killed on active service during WW II.

174. The twenty-six members of Ynysddu Boys' Brigade, with their officers in 1908. In modern times the pillbox hats have been replaced by more comfortable and acceptable headgear. Boys' Brigade companies still flourish in the area.

175. A scene from Bedwellty Show around 1909. Arthur Edwards (on left) enjoys his pint after running in a race. In the early 1900s Arthur farmed Castell - Cwrw. Wyllie village now stands on the land that belonged to this farm.

176. Important guests with Lord Tredegar when Bedwellty Show was held at Risca on 2 September 1912. At this time, and until comparatively recently, the show was always held on the first Monday in September.

177. This float, named 'The Roaring 20s', from a mid-1970s carnival, shows Lulu's Toppers.

178. In 1911 the building housing the Pontllanfraith Schools was almost completely destroyed by fire. This photograph shows local dignitaries gathered for the ceremony of laying the foundation stone for rebuilding which started almost immediately.

179. The Cwmfelinfach/Ynysddu Carnival in 1947. To the right are Councillor Mrs Withers and Mr Morgan.

180. Heads and senior teachers from the Blackwood area on a visit to Crookham, Aldershot, in July 1961.

181.   Rev H E Bates leads the Sunday School members of the Central Methodist Church along Blackwood High Street as part of the Whitsun Anniversary Procession in the early 1950s. The Red and White Services' office is now used by Darlows.

182.   The Committee and Officials of Oakdale Rugby Club in 1936.

183. Wyllie Colliery Officials on an outing to Cheddar Caves, 1955. From the left: David Edwards, David Minton, John Fox (Manager), Dai Davies, Jack Prescott, Bill Bennett, Ernie Price, Tom Brazier, Jim Pritchard, Cliff Evans, Jack Edwards, Jim Meredith, Reg Hunt, Unknown, Edgar Blakeman, Charlie Hughes and Bill Reed.

184. In 1917 this tank came to Blackwood to help to persuade people to buy Government stocks and so lend their money to the government to help pay for the war effort. These investments were some of the biggest confidence tricks ever perpetrated by a British Government. Not only did the government reduce the interest paid on War Loan from 5% to 3½% but it has never repaid the loan. The sale price today for every £100 loaned to the government at that time is less than £40. In those days £200 would buy a decent house in the area!

185. A happy group of mothers and children from the Penllwyn on a day out to Porthcawl c 1930.

186. June Bennett, the Carnival Queen, at the Coronation celebrations in 1953 is seated in an Eisteddfod chair and surrounded by her four attendants who are Wendy Couzens, Sheila Laffan, Pauline Munday and Mary Jenkins.

187. This photograph, of the Blackwood Branch of the British Womens' Temperance Association was taken in the garden of Woodbine House, the home of Mr & Mrs Evan Jones. It is now the Woodbine Club. Back row: Miss Lewis, Mrs J Coleman, Mrs Geo Coleman, Mrs W C Woodward, Mrs Gregory and Mrs Bendall. Second row: Miss H Baskerville, Mrs Lewis, Miss Tucker, Mrs Richardson, Mrs J Hodge, Mrs Price, Mrs Jack Coleman, Mrs Tom Gibbs and Mrs M A Morgan. Third row: Mrs Sumption, Mrs D J Thomas, Mrs (Captain) Thomas, Mrs J V Lewis, Mrs Houseley, Mrs Crook, Mrs Hendy, Miss A Baskerville, Mrs Evans Jones and Mrs Hughes. Front row: Miss Bessie Morris, Miss Budding, Mrs Maud Jones, Mrs Jack Church, Mrs Parker, Mrs Lewis Lewis, Mrs A Stokes, Miss Nellie Lewis and Miss Annie Jones.

188. Off home for the last time! Parents collecting pupils from Blackwood Infants School, Cefn Road, on Wednesday 22 October, 1980. Pupils were moved to a new school behind Morrison Street. The old school was subsequently demolished and houses built on the site.

189. Victory Celebrations in 1945 on Albion Terrace, Blackwood. Standing: Delsie Morgan, May Harris, Brian Head, Marie Goodwin, Owen Parfitt, Eva Hopkins, Roger Head, M Griffiths, David Pask, M Harris, Alun Pask and Beattie Head. Sitting: Olive Morgan, B Matthews, Unknown, Maud Hudson, Unknown and Winnie Pask.

190. A Street Party held in Llanover Avenue, Penllwyn, to celebrate the Silver Jubilee of King George V and Queen Mary in 1935. To the right is W J Edwards, station master of Cwmfelinfach.

191. A queen and her attendants with a gathering, mainly of children and young people, outside the Baptist Chapel in Markham Cresent, Oakdale in the 1920s. Almost everyone, regardless of age, wears headgear.

192. A very early picture of The Pontllanfraith Hairdressers' float at what appears to be a carnival or agricultural meeting of some kind.

193. *Oklahoma* at Pontllanfraith Grammar Technical School, 1974-75. The cast included pupils belonging to the last sixth form at the school before it was reorganised into a comprehensive school. From this time sixth form studies were transferred to the Sixth Form College at Crosskeys.

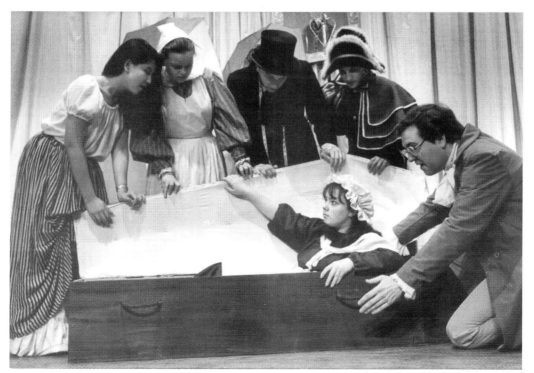

194. Mrs Sowerberry (Kirsty Thomas) taking a tumble into a coffin during Pontllanfraith Comprehensive School's production of *Oliver* at the school in 1992. The other members of the cast shown here are Charlotte (Christine Ung), Widow Corney (Ceri Williams), Mr Sowerberry (Ian Lilly), Mr Bumble (Mark Bunston) and Dr Grimwig (Mr Nigel Blunt).

195. Wyllie Village Ladies' Choir c 1952. Standing: A Shuck, T Brazier, M Minton, F Phillips, J Lewis, E Price, G Burgoyne, W Carpenter, Unknown, J Burgoyne, A Price, T Morgan, E James, T Litter, Unknown, G Price, Unknown and W Tucker. Seated: W Jones, M Edwards, Unknown, M Bayliss, M Edwards, J Jones, J Adams, J Snow, E Hardwicke and C Hughes. Kneeling: A Davies, M Butler, Unknown, Unknown, J Liddy, E Rees and B Thomas.

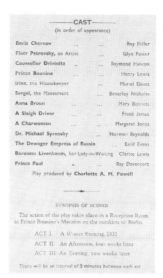

196. Blackwood Dramatic Society has a long and illustrious history. In the period immediately after the last war the society's players travelled the length and breadth of South Wales giving charity performances and competing in the Drama Week competitions that were held in almost every town. Sometimes they played three or four times in the same week. In Blackwood, while rehearsing in The Hut on Albion Terrace, they staged their productions at the Miners' Welfare Hall. Friday, 1st June 1956, was a great day for the society, for it saw the first performance in their own theatre. The play chosen was Marcelle Maurette's *Anastasia*. The play was produced by Charlotte Powell, a founder member of the society, and the cast included players that were to be the backbone of the society for decades. During the war the Primitive Methodist Church in Morris Lane, which had ceased to function as an active church before the war started, had been used as a storage centre for supplies that might be needed in an emergency. After the war was over it could be put to other use, and what better use than for an amateur dramatic society? The name of the society was subsequently changed to Blackwood Little Theatre and is still very active today.

197. The cast of *Anastasia* - the last of four plays in the season 1955-56, but the first play to be staged at Blackwood Little Theatre. Standing: Roy Fidler, Henry Lewis, Charlotte Powell, Glyn Foster, Ray Davenport, Norman Reynolds, Clarice Lewis, Mary Bennett, Frank James and Ray Hancox. Front row: Enid Evans, Margaret Jones and Gwyn Beard.

198. Blackwood Dramatic Society's production of *And So To Bed*. From the left: Portia West, Linda Bowditch, Archie Morgan, David Lawlor, Marjorie James, Glyn Foster, Flo James and Emlyn Hughes.

199. Strindberg, the Swedish dramatist and novelist, owes his greatest fame to his play *The Father*. This photograph shows the cast in Blackwood Little Theatre's production. Henry Lewis (centre) is in conversation with Marie Coggins and Eira Scandrett, while Wyndham Scandrett and other members of the cast look on.

200. Blackwood Operatic Society's production of The Merry Widow in 1974. From the back the ladies are: Unknown, Unknown, Jen Morgan, Unknown, Olga Williams, Rose Pope, Edith Davies, Marina Trace, Diane Payne and Edna Jenkins. The gentlemen from the left are: Keith Young, Mel Watts, Unknown, Tony Morgan, Keith Bather, Howard Davies, Ieuan Jenkins, Keith Williams and Peter Lynne.

201. Members of the chorus for Blackwood Operatics' production of *Viva Mexico* in 1979. Rear: Peter Lynne, Keith Williams, Caryl Thomas, Bryn Davies, Keith Bather and Krys Bather. Second row from the rear: Mary Price, Olga Williams, Audrey Phillips, Morfydd Phelps, June Davies, Ken Phillips and Pat Doolan. Third row: May Wallace, Betty Fisher, Pat Powell, Angela Harris, Monica Harris, Edgar Garland, Annette Parry and Andrea Ponsford. Behind: Mel Watts, Carol Humphries, Gwyneth Bryan and Roy Thomas. Front row: Judith Evans, Janet Berry, Pauline Lloyd, Mel Watts, Marina Trace, Gwyneth Greenslade and Gwyneth Ford.

202. Blackwood Ranger Guides 1977. Included are Linda Maguire, Sian Ballard, Martine Monk, Bronwen Pugh, Ann Maguire, Kim Arnold and Judith Lloyd.

203. Members of the Central Methodist Church walk along Blackwood High Street in the 1950s. Their organist and choirmaster, D M Williams walks alongside. In the background the businesses are, from the right, Melias (Grocer), Norman Lewis (Dentist), The Beauty Parlour, Dorothy Goodwin (The Wool Shop), Tomkins (Newsagent), D J Evans (Grocer), Jordans (Shoes) and Resteghini's Cafe.

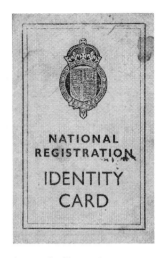

204.   There is much discussion at present about the pros and cons of Identity Cards. During the last war everyone was supplied with an identity card similar to the one shown here. Even today many people who lived through those times can quote their identity number. I remember mine - XOFA 1333! The letters signified a geographical area, the first three figures were allocated to the house and the last figure to an individual in the house according to that person's seniority.

205.   Prize Day at Pontllanfraith Comprehensive School in 1984. An important day in the life of the school for the guest speaker was Miss (now Dame) Margaret Price, a former pupil of Pontllanfraith Grammar School. Also included in the photograph are the Head Girl, Head Boy and Mr E J Maguire, the headmaster. Margaret Price was born in Tredegar and with much encouragement from her father began her musical studies at Trinity College, London, where she won a number of awards including the Elizabeth Schuman Prize. She made her operatic debut in 1962 playing Cherubino in the Welsh National Opera's production of *The Marriage of Figaro*. The following year saw her tread the boards at Covent Garden. She has become one of the leading interpreters of Mozart, singing at all the great opera houses throughout the world with the leading conductors and singers of the day. Margaret Price was made a CBE in 1982 and awarded an honorary doctorate of music by the University of Wales in 1983.

206./207   Mynyddislwyn Male Voice Choir - 1990

Back row, left to right: Jehoida Jones, Keith Jones, Dennis Morgan, Alan Matthews, Frank Shore, Stan Hughes, Tom Mortimer, Michael Butler, Ray Owen, Peter Hughes and Alan Mills. Third row: Tom Edwards, Derek Andrews, Sid Thomas, Glyn Morgan, Horace Hammett, David Rideout, John Cribb, Tom Davies, John Morris, Stewart Locke, Michael Crandon and Len Sutor. Second row: Harry Riley, Roy Sterry, Wyn Powell, Dewi Llewellyn, Gerald French, Ron Wright, Tony Edwards, Graham Greenslade, Islwyd Davies and Jack Lewis. Front row: Walter Bennett, Eric Gwilt, Ray Clarke, Joe Tiakiacs, John Jones, John Porter, Trevor Prankerd, Richard Bourton (*Pianist*), Paul James (*Conductor*) and Christopher Hawker (*Chairman*).

Back row, left to right: Alan Mills, Vernon Jones, Roy Jones, Glyn Millard, Godfrey Williams, Danny Morgan, Sid James, Tom Griffiths, Ken Tuck and John Wynne. Third row: Charlie Weaver, Arthur Jones, Trevor Trace, Cyril Thomas, Trevor Davies, Les Herring, Aneurin Bevan, Terry Toms and Ray Payne. Second row: Delwyn Price, David Jones, Jim Pritchard, Trevor Price, John Portsmouth, Jack Cook, John Gibbs, Roy Thompson, Brian Totterdale, Peter Reynolds and John Matthews. Front row: Arthur Griffiths, Idris Thomas, Don Cook, Elwyn Price, John Hawkins, Ron Coleman, Eddie Bevan, Clarrie Grey, Ken Roberts and Don Rowe.

Mynyddislwyn Male Voice Choir was founded in 1967 by the members of Wyllie Gleemen. In the early years it was often difficult to get the members together for practice because so many of them were employed in the coal and steel industries, two industries that demanded shift work. With the demise of these industries getting members together to practice has got a little easier. Consequently the size of the choir has continued to grow and today there are about 90 members. The choir used to meet for practice in Libanus School but has recently bought Penmain Chapel and converted it for their own use. All concerts are given in aid of charity, the Annual Concert taking place locally every year in May. A Ladies' Section was formed in 1972 to help in fundraising. Anyone interested in joining can make enquiries at the former Penmain Chapel any Monday or Thursday evening.

208. Members of Pontllanfraith Rotary Club with Ray Young, their first president. Pontllanfraith Rotary Club was formed by Mike Jones, John Kajzer-Hughes, Lewis Jenkins, David McLain and Ray Young, as a result of a meeting held at The Ivor Arms on 22 April, 1984. The Inaugural Dinner was held at Maes Manor on 1 October 1984. Very quickly they increased their numbers to thirty and moved to their now permanent home at Bryn Meadows. During their first decade they have raised tens of thousands of pounds for charity. The money has come by organising Businessmen's Lunches, Marathon Walks, Duck and Mouse Races, etc. Some of the good causes for which this money has been used are providing guide dogs for blind people, making donations to the St David's Cancer Research, Polio Plus and Water Aid, buying an electric chair for Ystrad Mynach Special Needs School and supplying a Junior School with a football kit. They have gathered together and taken medical supplies to Bosnia, Croatia and Poland. The club is twinned with the Rotary Club at St Jean-de-Luz and with clubs in Poland. They meet on Monday evenings.

FOUNDER MEMBERS

★

President:
RAY YOUNG .... Coalmining

Vice-President
RICHARD LEWIS .... Furniture Retailing

Junior Vice-President:
PETER REYNISH .... Licensed Victualling

Honorary Secretary:
DAVID GRIFFITH .... General Law Practice

Honorary Treasurer:
GEOFF WATERS .... Taxation Consultancy Service

Members of Council:
DAVID BROUGHTON .... Fruit and Vegetable Wholesaling
DAVID EDWARDS .... Civil Engineering
IAN GOODENOUGH .... Architecture
ALLAN MARTIN .... Switchgear Manufacturing
ALAM SABAH .... General Medical Service
ALLAN SATTERTHWAITE .... Electricity Supply Service

Members:
DAVID CHAPMAN .... Mechanical Engineering
ROBERT DODDS .... Business Statistics
GRAHAM HILDITCH .... Horticulture
LEW JENKINS .... Electrical Installation Service
TED JONES .... Surveying
JOHN KAJZER-HUGHES .... Automobile Servicing
RAY KING .... Coalmining Engineering
MIKE LOCKE .... Plumbing and Central Heating Service
JEFFREY LUXTON .... Accountancy
KERRY McCARTHY .... Assurance Life
DAVID McLAIN .... Electronic Components Manufacturing
STEVE MORGAN .... Security Alarms Systems
BILL PARSONS .... Local Government Engineering
JOHN PRICE .... Electrical Equipment Manufacturing
KEITH REES .... Mining Equipment Maintenance
JOHN THOMAS .... Postal Service
HAYDN WELCH .... Higher Education

209. Members and supporters of Pontllanfraith Rotary Club on the completion of their drive in a Sinclair C5 electric mini car from John O'Groats to Land's End. The drive broke the existing record for this journey (using an electric car) by 10 hours and raised over £11,000 for charity. The most lasting memory of most of the drivers is 'If you have a death wish, drive a C5!'

210. The earliest known photograph (early 1930s) of Markham & District Colliery Band taken with their trophies in front of the Institute at Markham. The band is still very much alive and meet at their Bandroom in the Showfield, Blackwood on Mondays and Fridays.

211. Members of a fishing club outside the Hollybush Inn, Hollybush in the early 1960s. Records show that this inn was used as an alehouse in 1820 but it is probable that it was built some years before this. For a period a room at the front was used for religious services. Coal was mined in the area from the early part of the last century and in 1868 E D Williams of Maesrhuddud bought the nearby Hollybush Colliery. Colliers worked 10 hour shifts for 22/- (£1.10) a week. E D Williams built houses and a schoolroom in 1874. A new school was built on the main road in 1918 and demolished in 1995.

212. An old photograph of miners with their boss at Hollybush Colliery.

213./214. Blackwood High Street in 1910, looking north from a point in front of the Forresters. The horse and cart is passing Sumptions the Chemists, to the right of which is the business of J V Lewis. J T Broad, Surgeon Dentist has premises above and is open from 10 a.m. to 6.30 p.m. Men can be seen high above the pavement, attending to problems with the telephone wires. Today the scene has changed significantly. The drapery store in the centre has been replaced by Argos following a serious fire comparatively recently, the telephone wires have gone underground and the motorcar has replaced the horse and cart.

215./216. Blackwood High Street in 1938, looking south from a point in front of the present day Post Office. On the left is B Griffiths the draper with D J Evans the grocer next door. The distant white building is the Parrot Hotel which has been replaced by the Library. The double frontage building on the far side of Bridge Street was taken down to widen the road. Apart from those mentioned all the original buildings are extant.

217./218. Commercial Street, Ynysddu in 1912, when on the main highway linking Pontllanfraith to Risca. The main road was to move to High Street, taking the Post Office with it, before finding its present route on the old railway line. Typical of so many streets in the older villages, the motorcar has taken priority in areas where children could formerly play in relative safety. New houses replace the old properties on the right.

Ivor Street, Pontllanfraith.

219./220. Today, this view of Ivor Street, Pontllanfraith is part ᴏꜰ ꜱ̲ ꜱ̲ ꜱ̲ ᴛ̲ road from Newport to Blackwood. At the time of the early photograph (c 1915) it was a ᴅᴏ̲ ꜱ̲ ᴅ̲ The main road to Newport was along Gelligroes Road, which is behind the houses on ᴛ̲ꜱ̲ ꜱ̲ᴛ. Apart from the pace of life suggested by the road surface and its accompanying modes of transport this scene remains relatively unchanged.

MKM 9   ABERNANT ROAD, MARKHAM.

Copyright
Frith's

221./2 A scene in Markham village in the 1950s. A Saxon & Co pop lorry delivers to __op. In the foreground is Markham Presbyterian Church which was taken down in the 1980s. The only church in Markham today is the Congregational Church. The scene is immediately recognisable yet has changed significantly.

Acknowledgements

Numerous people have helped in the production of this book, through their willingness to share information and by the provision of many old photographs. While every effort has been made to get at the truth, on occasions it has been difficult to separate fact from fiction. Any errors that occur must be considered wholly mine, and for these I apologise.

My grateful thanks are due to Mr John Watkins for checking text and to the undermentioned who kindly loaned original material, who helped to identify faces and places, and who provided dates and other interesting information.

Mr Gordon Bennett, Mrs Eluned Davies, Mr John Davies, Mr Colin Donovan, Mr Peter Downing, Mr Jack Edwards, Mr Jack Gardener, Mr Doug Gilchrist, Mr Robert Green, Mrs Pam Hillier, Mr & Mrs Henry Lewis, The Hollybush Inn, Mr E J Maguire, Mr Jack Morris, The officers of Mynyddislwyn Male Voice Choir, Mr Owen Parfitt, Mr & Mrs W J Price, Mrs Shirley Rees, Mrs Cheryl Robson, Mr Gary Rosser, Mr Gerry Thomas, Mr Malcolm Thomas, Mrs Joyce Thomas and Mr Ray Young. Sincere apologies are extended to anyone who may have been inadvertently omitted.

In particular I would like to thank Mr Gwilym Davies and Mr Malcolm Thomas of Old Bakehouse Publications, Abertillery. They initiated the book and have a kept a careful eye on things at every stage of its production. I must also thank all the staff at the publishers who have always been most courteous and helpful, and who have made many worthwhile suggestions.

The author would very much welcome the loan of any unpublished photographs, memorabilia, etc., from readers who might wish to see the material included in the third book in this series. He may be contacted through the publishers at the address given at the front of the book.

Further books in this series are available from Bookshops or through The Publishers.

Blaenavon Through The Years in Photographs   **- Volume 1**
by Malcolm Thomas and John Lewis   ISBN 0 9512181 0 7
Blaenavon Through The Years in Photographs   **- Volume 2**
by Malcolm Thomas and John Lewis   ISBN 0 9512181 3 1
Blaenavon Through The Years in Photographs   **- Volume 3**
by Malcolm Thomas and John Lewis   ISBN 1 874538 10 7
Old Aberbeeg and Llanhilleth in Photographs   **- Volume 1**
by Bill Pritchard   ISBN 0 9512181 5 8
Old Aberbeeg and Llanhilleth in Photographs   **- Volume 2**
by Bill Pritchard   ISBN 1 874538 35 2
Blackwood Yesterday in Photographs   **- Book 1**
by Ewart Smith   ISBN 0 9512181 6 6
A Look at Tredegar in Photographs   **- Volume 1**
by Philip Prosser   ISBN 0 9512181 4 X
A Portrait of Rhymney   **- Volume 1**
by Marion Evans   ISBN 1 874538 40 9
A Portrait of Rhymney   **- Volume 2**
by Marion Evans   ISBN 1 874538 70 0
Brynmawr, Beaufort and Blaina in Photographs   **- Volume 1**
by Malcolm Thomas   ISBN 1 874538 15 8
Caldicot and the Villages of the Moor   **- Volume 1**
by Malcolm D Jones   ISBN 1 874538 50 6
Talgarth - Jewel of the Black Mountains   **- Volume 1**
by Roger G. Williams   ISBN 1 874538 60 3
Remember Abergavenny   **- Volume 1**
by Louis Bannon   ISBN 1 874538 75 1
Trinant in Photographs   **- Volume 1**
by Clive Daniels   ISBN 1 874538 80 8

Also available are novels of local interest which include:
The Black Domain - *by Ralph Thomas*   ISBN 0 9512181 7 4
A portrayal of life and romance in 19th century industrial Blackwood with a balanced blend of fact and fiction.
The Land of Brychan - *by Nansi Selwood*   ISBN 1 874538 30 1
Set in 17th century Brecknock and Glamorgan, this is a novel full of richness of the life of the gentry class based on a fusion of fact and folk memory.
Folklore of Blaenau Gwent   ISBN 1 874538 85 9
A fascinating and definitive collection of centuries old legends and folklore from northern Monmouthshire.